DEDICATION

Questo libro lo dedico a mia Mamma Rosa,
che e con Angeli adesso.

This book is dedicated to my Mama Rosa,
who is with the Angels now.

Cento Anni

ONE HUNDRED YEARS OF
MORELLI'S ICE CREAM

Published 2011 by
Colourpoint Books
Colourpoint House, Jubilee Business Park
Jubilee Road, Newtownards, BT23 4YH
Tel: 028 9182 6339
Fax: 028 9182 1900
E-mail: info@colourpoint.co.uk
Web: www.colourpoint.co.uk

First Edition
First Impression

A catalogue record for this book is available from the British Library.

Designed by April Sky Design, Newtownards
Tel: 028 9182 7195
Web: www.aprilsky.co.uk

Printed by W&G Baird, Antrim

ISBN 978-1-906578-97-8

Cento Anni
ONE HUNDRED YEARS OF
MORELLI'S ICE CREAM

DANIELA MORELLI

CONTENTS

Cento Anni
Introduction

A question I'm often asked is "are you Irish or Italian?" and my answer is always the same, "I don't know". I'm a nomad. I was born here in Ireland, as were both of my parents. Technically, that would make me Irish. Well, actually technically that would make me British as I was born in Northern Ireland. I have an Italian name, I look Italian, yet I don't speak Italian. So when I'm in Ireland I'm Italian and when I go to Italy, I'm Irish. Confused?

As a child I always remember feeling different, but I couldn't really figure out why. Perhaps I was too young to realise that, compared to my friends, my name was a little different. At school I got called "Smelly Morelli", although I don't think that upset me to any great degree and I'm sure I gave as good as I got.

My earliest memories are very fond ones. I made my first 'poke' around the age of three and later progressed to standing on a wooden crate behind the counter pouring minerals from the coke machine. My childhood wasn't spent doing the things normal kids do like watching cartoons or playing with Barbie dolls. Instead, I spent long summers hanging around our ice cream factory pestering my poor father and brothers into letting me help make the ice cream. I recall being locked in the walk-in deep freeze at least twice. As I got older, my responsibilities grew and by the time I was sixteen, I was in charge of a shift in my parents shop 'Cappuccinos' in Portrush. It was a lot of responsibility, but I think that experience was invaluable to me now. I have always been a 'people' person and my time working in the shop and growing up at the same time was special.

Friends always comment on how nice it is that my family all work together in the family business and tell me that they wish they could do the same. As anyone who is involved in family business can testify, it isn't great all the time. You definitely need a thick skin, and being a female in a traditional Italian family, it's sometimes difficult to gain the benefit of the doubt when you're throwing your ideas into the wrath of a male forum. On a more positive note, there is the advantage of continual support (most of the time) and what one sibling lacks, the other usually makes up for. At the end of the day, we all have the same objective and that is to keep our business a success and maintain our reputation.

One thing that each and every member of my family has in common is a huge sense of pride when it comes to the family business. We have it good compared to what my grandparents had to put up with when they first got here. There is a great sense of accomplishment amongst the fourth and even fifth generations of the family that we have reached our *Cento Anni* (One hundred years).

My family's story is just like the perfect ice cream recipe. It has been blended together with love, hardship, family strength and Italian passion. It begins in the idyllic village of Casalattico in Italy and continues on the North Coast of Northern Ireland. Allow me to take you through the twists and turns, and introduce you to the colourful characters and the fascinating string of events that is the Morelli Story.

Daniela Morelli

Note to Reader: *In some instances I have referred to Angelo and Anastasia as Nonno and Nonna. These are the Italian words for Grandmother and Grandfather, and that of course is what I called them.*

Leila (my niece) enjoying a Morelli's ice cream.

CHAPTER ONE

Where it all began

Dove Cominció

Casalattico is a special place held in the hearts of many people. It's believed that up to 8,000 Irish Italians have ancestors or family roots here. Geographically, Casalattico is located about 110km Southeast of Rome. It's a mountainous region in the province of Frosinone. With a population of around 800 inhabitants, it's a small place but it certainly has a big character.

I'm privileged to be able to go back to Italy at least once a year to visit. Each and every member of my family usually goes too, bringing their own children, friends and families. I can't describe the feeling I get when I go back to Italy. It's such a special place filled with breathtaking scenery, colourful characters and of course rustic food and plentiful local wine. It seems like a different world made special by knowing that the roots of my family belong here. It's greatly enjoyed by all who visit and everybody has a story or two to tell when they return.

Casalattico is a quiet place, except for in July and August when the community swells somewhat with ex-pat families coming back to enjoy their holidays. The square in Casal is a popular meeting point as the piazza is home to the Church of San Barbato and a fabulous pizzeria which serves its authentic pizza alfresco. You can enjoy the panoramic views of the valley whilst sipping a glass of local *vino rosso* (red wine).

Casalattico has many different hamlets, and the Morelli family home is in San Andrea, a small hamlet of around twelve dwellings at the foot of the *Valle di Comino* (Comino valley). San Andrea has a restaurant called *'C'era Una Volta'* (Once upon a time), which serves some of the best rustic home cooked Italian food in the province. There is also a bar called 'Mundial', which is always a great place to hook up with friends and partake in a game of *bocce* (the Italian version of bowls) which is taken very seriously!

Naturally, it's a very different place today compared with what it was like many years ago when my grandparents were growing up. Being a rural area, there was little work for anyone and the only work available to them was agricultural. In the late nineteenth and early twentieth centuries, a significant number of young people left Casalattico and its surrounding areas to seek work in Ireland, Scotland, England, France and even as far a field as the USA.

My great-grandfather Barbato Morelli and my great-grandmother Maria-Celeste (nee Matassa), originally lived in the village of Le Lesche, about a mile from San Andrea. Barbato had eight brothers, Giacomo, Vincenzo, Annunziato, Antonio, Giuseppe, Constantino, Domenico and Pietro or Peter as he would later be known. The family owned several small patches of land which they cultivated and tried to make a living from by producing olives and other produce, but it wasn't enough. Eventually, several of the brothers made the decision to leave their home to seek work and opportunities abroad.

There was much talk around this time of local people leaving to seek employment elsewhere and being successful. Making the decision to leave was extremely tough, but for so many, including my great-uncles, staying behind was simply not an option. So with rumours of jobs and money proving fruitful for others elsewhere, the brothers left for their big adventure.

It's not clear how the brothers separated, but I do know that Peter ended up in Paris and was given a job in a factory as a glass blower. He continued to blow glass for a while and had a natural talent for it. The young Peter was then offered a position in another glass factory just outside London, which he accepted. Peter continued with this trade, but after a while found that it was beginning to damage his health by effecting his breathing and lungs. He gave up and proceeded to travel to Northern Ireland where he knew that his brother Giuseppe (Joe) had set up a business.

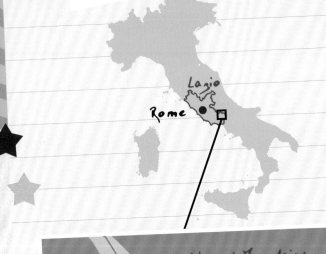

The Church of San Barbato (St Barbato), Casalattico.

Pietro (Peter) Morelli

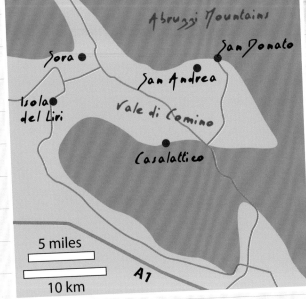

Casalattico

Family composite picture.

From left to right, Back: Pietro (Peter), Giacomo, Vincenzo, Annunziato, Antonio and Guiseppe.

Front: Domenico, Barbato, Clementina (parent), Constantino and Onorio (parent).

The Morelli family home in San Andrea.

CHAPTER TWO

Pastures New
Nuovi Grizzonti

Upon reaching Northern Ireland, Peter found himself helping his brother Joe, who had established a café in Ballymena. He worked extremely hard for him for a full summer season. At the end of that season, Peter had expected to get either a share of the profits or perhaps a share of the business, but was rewarded with little more than a pat on the back from Joe. He didn't resent his brother for this, but instead, realised that it was time to leave the comfort of his brother's bosom and go it alone.

Peter travelled further north and settled in Coleraine late in 1910. He soon established his own business in 1911 at Stone Row, a street just off The Diamond. It was a café selling fish and chips as well as sweets, tobacco and ice cream and it quickly became very popular with the locals. It was quite a small, dark shop, but it gave Peter a living. It was also his own business and that was what really mattered to him. He found the Coleraine people easy to get along with and settled in well, working hard to build up his little shop. He was eventually able to employ some staff to help with the work load.

Not long after this, Peter met and fell in love with Annie Dymond, a local woman from Coleraine who captured his heart. They married and both of them worked in the shop for many years. Everything was going well for Peter and he was looking to expand his business. In 1914 he did just that and established a second shop, the 'Ice Palace', on the promenade in Portstewart. It was of course double the work, but now that Annie was helping, Peter could manage the two shops well.

Although ice cream was a feature at the Stone Row shop, it didn't sell in any great quantity, but Portstewart was different. People seemed to love the stuff there and couldn't get enough. Peter had been given the family ice cream recipe by his father and although it was delicious, it was a very labour intensive process making it.

The process was very, very difficult. There was no electricity at that time in Coleraine, but there was in Portstewart. There were no fridges and obviously no freezers so the ice cream had to be made using ice and salt for the freezing process. Blocks of ice would be brought down from Belfast on the train to Portstewart's Cromore station which was a halt between Coleraine and Portrush. There was a tram that left Portstewart station and made its way down the Cromore Road and right along the promenade. Peter would accompany the block of ice on the tram and used a make-shift trolley to carry it to the shop, where he quickly brought it out to the back yard and covered it to stop it from melting.

The liquid ice cream mixture would then be poured into a metal can made from zinc, with a wooden tub surrounding it. In the space between the can and the wooden tub, he poured ice and salt. The mixture froze inside by the continual stirring of the ice and salt, but it took a lot of effort and a lot of stirring to get it to freeze. Not an ideal way to make anything, but it had to be done and the extra effort was rewarded by the ice cream's soaring popularity.

Peter happily continued to expand both businesses and he and Annie were kept very busy. Each summer they became busier and busier, which allowed them to save for their future. Peter felt very at home on the North Coast as he had finally found a new home, a new life and an ideal wife. Although he missed Italy, he was very happy with his new situation.

CENSUS OF IRELAND, 1911.

Two Examples of the mode of filling up this Table are given on the other side.

FORM A.

From left to right:
Peter Morelli, Annie
Dymond (Morelli) and
Giacomo Morelli.

Census form from 1911
showing Peter and Annie
Dymond.

Peter and Annie with two members of staff at the first Morelli's in Stone Row, Coleraine, c.1911.

CHAPTER THREE

The Emerald Isle
L'Isola Verde

Barbato Morelli, my great-grandfather and Peter's brother, had lost his leg to gangrene, Due to his affliction he didn't join his brothers in their mass departure from Italy. Instead he and his wife made a home in Casalattico. His wife Maria Celeste was however keen to support her husband and young son Angelo (my grandfather), and when an opportunity presented itself to her, she grabbed it with both hands.

Her brother Antonio had been in Dublin for a while and he offered to help Maria Celeste set up her own business in Parnell Street in 1915. After things settled and she found her feet in business, she gathered enough money to allow her husband and son make the journey to Dublin to join her. Barbato and Angelo arrived in Dublin in 1916, just before the Easter Rising.

With the rebellion breaking out in Dublin just after their arrival, one can only imagine the anguish and fear that my Grandfather experienced. He and the family sought refuge in the basement of the shop in Parnell Street, rarely getting a breath of fresh air until the rebellion was over. As strangers in a foreign

country, and after such a violent welcome to that new country and way of life, Maria and Barbato decided that it was no place for their 9 year old boy and arranged for Angelo to travel north, safe in the knowledge that he would be looked after by Peter and Annie.

Angelo spent almost three years in Coleraine where he went to school as a border at the Ursuline Convent or the Loreto as it's known today. In 1919, Barbato accompanied Angelo back to Italy, where he continued his education at the local schools near his home village of Casalattico. Once he had finished his education, he soon realised that opportunities and jobs where very scarce at home and he too decided, just like his uncles, to leave Italy again.

It was a natural choice for Angelo to return to Coleraine. Peter and Annie hadn't had any children of their own, so Angelo began his employment at the Ice Palace in Portstewart and although it was a tough apprenticeship, Angelo found his feet very quickly and grew into his new job admirably. Angelo learned every aspect of the business, paying close attention to detail. He didn't want to let his parents down. He worked hard for his Uncle and eventually, his responsibilities grew. Angelo was a natural and had a good way with the customers. His only distraction was of back home and thoughts of his childhood sweetheart Anastasia. Angelo had made an inward promise to himself that he would marry that girl, and with a bit of hard work and determination, that was exactly what he did.

It was very apparent that Angelo was ambitious, and a profound thinker. He had thought deeply about his future and he worked out ways to get what he wanted. Upon reaching the age of twenty-one, Angelo gathered the courage to ask Peter to sell him the business in Portstewart. Angelo had virtually no money of his own, but as I said, he had thought this through and even persuaded his father to write to Peter to convince him to sell Angelo the shop to give him a start in life and a business of his own. Eventually, Peter agreed, but at a price. Angelo took over the shop in 1928 and had to repay his Uncle £600 for the Goodwill of the business. He agreed to pay him in instalments. Peter had decided that his idea of instalments was different from Angelo's. Let's just say that Peter had a reputation in the family for being frugal! Angelo assumed that at the end of each season, he would give Peter a certain amount of money and retain enough to be able to carry on for the next season, but Peter had other ideas. Being a hard task master, Peter would come to Angelo every weekend to collect the money and leave Angelo enough to buy stock for the following week. This went on for three full seasons until the debt was paid back. Angelo re-named the Ice Palace 'The Lido'.

Angelo didn't have time for any hobbies or interests, which was just as well as he couldn't afford them until his debt to Peter was repaid. He couldn't afford to employ a big staff either. Initially he had only one person helping him in the shop, but gradually, as time went on and the business became more established, he was able to take on more staff. He managed to save around £300 over time and in 1931 he decided to venture back to Casalattico in the hope of marrying the beautiful Anastasia.

CHAPTER FOUR

Unfinished Business
Affari da risolvere

Like Angelo, Anastasia Cassoni was born and raised in Casalattico. She lost her mother when she was only eight years old. She was the eldest of three and therefore took on the role of looking after her father and two younger siblings, sister Lidia and brother Nicola. The Cassoni family ran a grocery shop in Casalattico. Anastasia's father Amedeo was the manager of the local tax office and bank. She often helped her father in the office too.

Angelo was a frequent visitor to the Cassoni family home as he was very good friends with Nicola. They had bonded through a shared interest of music. Angelo would play the mandolin and sing whilst Nicola would accompany him on the violin or guitar. The pair would often perform in the piazza in the evenings for the local residents. These social occasions were a great excuse for Angelo to spend time with Anastasia and perhaps sparked that first feeling of love between the pair.

Angelo had always admired Anastasia, not only for her good looks, but also for her personable nature. She was loved by everybody. Perhaps he also saw her entrepreneurial spirit as having something

in common with him. As with everything back then, their courtship was somewhat parochial. Anastasia's father was very strict, so much so that they were not even permitted to walk beside each other in public. When I used to ask Nonno about his courting days he would describe it as 'Victorian'.

Angelo had been very shrewd about his intentions to marry Anastasia. He knew that her father was quite traditional and wouldn't grant his permission for the couple to get married unless he had enough money saved to give his daughter a good start in their married life. Angelo accelerated the process by saving enough money in Portstewart so that he could ask his permission as quickly as possible. At first Amedeo Cassoni was not too keen on the idea. Surprisingly, not because of his finances, but because he thought Angelo was too young to get married. At twenty-three, Angelo knew in his own mind exactly what he wanted, and at this stage he simply was not going to take no for an answer. He persevered and eventually Amedeo granted his permission. The couple were very much in love and in 1931 they were married in the Church of San Barbato in Casalattico.

After the wedding, Angelo and Anastasia prepared for the trip back to Portstewart to begin their journey as man and wife. For Anastasia, her new life was a daunting experience. She didn't speak any English, and upon their arrival, a feeling of depression enveloped Angelo, as he was apprehensive about how his new bride would settle in to her new environment. Their living accommodation was modest, a little flat above the shop with a few bits of furniture that he had managed to gather before he left for Italy, but their love was strong and that was all that really mattered.

Settling very quickly, Anastasia soon became extremely fond of Portstewart and made firm friendships, some of which lasted for the duration of her lifetime. I have very fond memories of my Nonna. She had the kindest of natures and had a very special bond with children. She was fantastic cook, and she had a wit that would out-smart the artful dodger. As you will soon discover, Anastasia was not only the matriarch of the Morelli family, but she also the matriarch of the Morelli family business. Without her, the story I'm telling would be a very different one.

Anastasia Cassoni, Casalattico, c.1928.

Anastasia Cassoni, c.1929.
The writing in the bottom
left corner reads, "Alla Cara
Mia Anastasia" (Anastasia,
My love).

Anastasia and Angelo, the bride and groom, 5 February 1931.

The building that once housed the Cassoni family's grocery shop in Casalattico.

Angelo and Anastasia's wedding, 1931, pictured outside the family home in San Andrea. The initials 'BM' at the top of the door stand for Barbato Morelli.

CHAPTER FIVE

A New Life
Una Nuova Vita

As Italians living in Northern Ireland, some would say that perhaps Angelo and Anastasia had the best of both worlds, and they certainly did. They were surrounded by an air of curiosity of sorts, as they were obviously very different from anyone in business in Portstewart at that time. However, they didn't see this as an obstacle, as they were welcomed into the community and fitted in quite well with the local people. Their shop became a popular meeting place for local families, groups of friends and business people, as well as visitors to the seaside town.

Anastasia was a very dedicated worker and she greatly enjoyed serving behind the counter and talking with her customers. This helped her to learn English and she also built up a warm rapport with the customers, which encouraged them to come back often. The local lads were particularly keen to pay a visit to The Lido to catch a glimpse of the beautiful Italian girl and although Angelo was a little jealous of the attention his wife was attracting, he realised that it was good for business and made no complaints.

As time went on, Anastasia became more comfortable in her new community and before long she was expecting their first child. Baby boy Nino was born in 1932 at number 1 Carlisle Road in Londonderry, where Anastasia's Aunt Julia was living. Anastasia went there to have her first child because she felt more comfortable with family and, most importantly, with someone who could also speak Italian. A second boy called Corrado arrived in 1933 and Guido completed the trio in 1935.

Anastasia and Angelo naturally had their hands full with three young boys and a business, but this was a role that Anastasia relished. She bonded immediately with her boys and gave each one her undivided love and attention, whilst still managing to keep her eye on the shop and make sure everything was running like clockwork. It was her nature to keep everything running smoothly. They managed perfectly but found the summer seasons a little difficult, when the shop became extremely busy. In the summer of 1935 Angelo's parents Barbato and Maria Celeste came from Italy to pay a visit and to help to look after the boys. This gave the couple the time they needed to spend in the shop working and building up their little empire. Unfortunately, during that visit Barbato passed away suddenly at the age of only sixty-one. This was naturally an upsetting time for the family. Barbato was laid to rest in Portstewart and Maria Celeste stayed for a while to consider her future.

She didn't feel at home in Portstewart and made her feelings clear to Angelo that she wanted to return to Casalattico. Angelo and Anastasia decided to send Nino and Corrado back to Italy with Maria Celeste. This decision was two-fold. Angelo wanted his mother to have some company and he also had a strong desire for his boys to know their Italian roots and learn the Italian language. When they arrived in Casalattico, Nino and Corrado were enrolled in a Kindergarten School that was run by the Compostrini order of nuns. They picked up the language very quickly and Nino recalls, "We were sad to leave our parents, but we were so excited about going to Italy with our grandmother. When we arrived, we went to school as borders and that wasn't very pleasant".

Guido, who was just a baby, remained in Portstewart with his parents. They carried on working and continually tried to improve the business by introducing new ideas. By doing most of the work in the shop themselves, they were able to save some money and in 1939, Angelo, Anastasia and Guido went back to Italy to visit Nino and Corrado. Angelo was also anxious to see his mother and to check that she was coping without her husband. It was in 1939 that the rumours started. Rumours of an impending war between Germany and France and England.

Unsure of what to do, Angelo and Anastasia thought about it and decided that it was best to return to Portstewart and their business immediately. They left Nino and Corrado behind because Italy was showing no signs at all of entering into the war.

As the couple made their way back to Portstewart with Guido, they were unusually detained for a short time in Rome. They had been mistakenly been classified Jewish by a gentleman in charge of all citizens travelling abroad. They had to prove they were not Jewish before being released. Eventually, they were released and permitted to continue their journey back to Northern Ireland.

Nino's Christening in Londonderry 1932.
From left to right, Front: Angelo, Anastasia, Midwife and baby
Nino. Back: Mario and Giuseppa Morelli (godparents).

Angelo and Anastasia in 1931
after their return to Portstewart.

Anastasia, baby Corrado, Angelo and Nino, c.1933.

Portstewart c.1933.
From left to right: Barbato,
Nino, Anastasia and Angelo.

From left to right:
Corrado, Anastasia,
Guido, Angelo, Maria
Celeste and Nino,
c.1938.

CHAPTER SIX

Trouble Ahead

Problemi all' orizzonte

Back in July 1931, Angelo had been asked to help when a close friend of Mussolini's named Balboa was undertaking a historic flight to America. The aircraft made a stop at Lough Foyle to re-fuel and because he spoke Italian, Angelo went along to translate. This event carried a rather high media profile and Angelo's part in this event would be remembered for all the wrong reasons. Both of my grandparents were the sort of people who never refused a plea for help and this worked sometimes to their detriment.

As they arrived back in Portstewart from their trip, the atmosphere was completely different from when they left only a short time before. There was much talk of the impending war, and although they had made a home and a successful business in Portstewart, they were terrified about what was going to happen. Angelo listened closely to the unfolding events both in Italy and in Britain and he feared the worse. He didn't want to unsettle Anastasia or make her worry so he didn't talk to her about his fears. However, being an astute woman, she knew deep down that there would be trouble

ahead. They felt uneasy and knew that if Italy joined the war effort, they would suddenly become enemies within a previously friendly community.

Mussolini was beginning to forge alliances with Nazi Germany and Italy joined forces and declared war on Britain on 10 June 1940. The 'trouble' came knocking on Angelo's door shortly after that at five o'clock one morning. A local police sergeant picked him up and took him to the local barracks. From there he was eventually transported to Belfast's Crumlin Road jail where he stayed for a week with other 'enemy aliens'. The truth of the matter was that Angelo was prepared for this. He had his bags packed. A gut feeling or instinct that he had hoped was wrong had come true and during that period in Crumlin Road, he did a lot of thinking and worrying. He worried for his sons in Italy; he worried for his dear wife who had been left behind alone with young Guido and most of all he worried that he wouldn't make it back again.

I had often wondered why Peter Morelli hadn't been taken also, but it was only when I was doing some research for this project that I came across

an important document. He had applied for British citizenship and had been issued with his 'Certificate of Naturalisation' in 1938. This meant that he was safe from the authorities. Perhaps he too had a 'gut feeling' about the unfolding events.

I would often ask Nonno about this time in his life expecting him to be full of bitter memories, but to my surprise, the opposite was true. He told me that although he felt terribly sad about his family being separated he never felt any animosity towards the British. To a certain degree, his loyalties were divided between his homeland and the country that had shown him sincere hospitality when he had first arrived. Being a methodical character, he learned to make the best out of a bad situation.

During his incarceration, some of Angelo's compatriots had chosen to join the ranks of the allies as a means of escaping, but he never considered this as an option. He was too frightened about how that could affect his two sons who were still in Italy. He went in as a civilian and he wanted to be released as a civilian.

Angelo had hoped that his family in Italy would be safe. He had consoled himself with the knowledge that that region in Italy was of very little military significance, but as the war raged in Italy, the region was in fact becoming central to the conflict. The near by area of Monte Casino had been heavily fortified by the Germans who were determined to make an advance on Rome. During

this time, the Morelli family home in San Andrea was commandeered by the Germans as their headquarters. Nino and Corrado were permitted to remain with their grandmother in the house, but were only allowed to use one room. The Germans had evacuated the whole village at this stage and it was quite an experience for two young boys. They both recall some very vivid memories of this time. One incident saw their grandmother wielding a machete at a German SS Captain! The Captain had lifted Corrado up on to the back of a lorry and she thought he was taking him away. The Captain had tears in his eyes and Corrado didn't understand what was happening. He still doesn't understand why that happened.

Among all this chaos, Maria Celeste tried to keep things as normal as she could for Nino and Corrado. One morning she sent them for milk. This errand could have been the end of Corrado. He recalls, "we were walking along a country road and we walked passed three or four German Lorries full of petrol cans that were stacked at least twenty feet high; the Lorries drove past us and we heard a lot of noise and commotion, it sounded like planes. The Lorries stopped underneath some trees. I knew they were going to be attacked and I panicked, I didn't know what to do. Nino shouted at me to run with him underneath a bridge, but I got flustered and I ran underneath one of the Lorries. I quickly realised what was happening and ran very quickly under the bridge with Nino. I got there just in time, two minutes later the whole lot went up in flames. It was a very close call". I've often wondered if they managed to get the milk!

The boys, along with their grandmother, eventually got taken away from their home for their own safety. They were taken to Ferentino, on the way to Rome, and then further south along the Calabrian coast, staying in a little seaside town called Citta Della Del Capo. They had to travel through Casino and because the battle was still going on there, they had difficulty getting through. When they eventually got down to Calabria, they didn't know where to go. Nino and Corrado took odd jobs wherever they could. They would go and clean the fishing boats in exchange for a handful of fish. They had no money and almost no food. Nino recalls, "we used to get an allowance of 100g of bread each day. Our grandmother didn't eat the crusts, so she would save them for us and give them to us if we were really hungry. One day I was hungry so I found where she had hidden them and I ate the lot. Corrado wasn't very pleased that I did this and he was so angry with me that he took a home-made fork and threw it at me. It stuck right in my ankle and I was in agony." Corrado added, "we even did a stint as altar boys down there and we were so hungry we used to eat the communion bread". It's also from this time that my dear uncle Corrado developed a severe hatred for butter. Being so hungry and desperate for any sustenance he could get his hands on, a large portion of butter turned up and Corrado wasted no time at all in tucking in. After making himself violently ill, he resolved there and then never to eat butter again. To this day I can confirm that he indeed cannot look at, never mind eat butter, which disappointingly rules out ice cream. However, I can confirm that Nino and Guido have no such reaction and enjoy ice cream most days.

Back in Portstewart, things were not going well for Anastasia. She did her best to look after the shop and Guido but they were difficult times. Angelo's bank account had been frozen so Anastasia couldn't withdraw any money to buy goods for the shop. During rationing, she had to make do with whatever she could get and carry on. Suppliers soon stopped giving goods as she couldn't afford to pay. One gentleman, however, was extremely kind to Anastasia. A local greengrocer called James McClean had become a friend and Angelo and Anastasia would buy all of their groceries from him. He told Anastasia not to worry about the money, she could have whatever she wanted and she could pay him back in her own time. His generosity and kindness was never forgotten.

Guido recalls the time he spent with his mother. They became very close and developed a unique bond. He said, "I remember her speaking in Italian to me and I would always answer her in English, so we both learned from each other". He continues, "she used to put me into the bed on her side so when she got in, she would slide me over and the bed would be nice and warm for her. We had a very strong relationship and although she could be very honest and even brutal at times, I loved her very much".

Much to the amazement of everyone, Anastasia and Guido were sent away from Portstewart. She was considered to be an enemy alien and a risk to the Allied Naval base further along the North Coast. It was difficult to understand what threat she would have been, but she had to go. She feared that the shop would have to close but friends of the family rallied round to keep it open, and she sought solace in Portadown where her sister Lidia lived. Lidia's husband had also been sent away and was later interned with Angelo. Lidia had a son named Mario who was around the same age as Guido. These two cousins developed a special brotherly relationship forged on this time they spent together. We often joke that he is the 'fourth brother' and fondly call him *Zio* (uncle).

A woman called Alba Forte ran the Morelli's shop in Portstewart in Angelo and Anastasia's absence. Her parents lived in Portrush and the family came from the same area in Italy. Alba's father had assured Angelo that if anything were to happen, he would send one of his daughters to look after the shop, and true to his word Alba kept the shop open. Not only that, but with her at the helm, the business thrived. Alba was very beautiful and consequently, she attracted not just the ordinary soldiers, but their officers too. Alba's sisters would also help her in the shop and one of them ended up marrying an officer whom she met there.

After staying in Portadown for a month or so, Anastasia was still not permitted to return to Portstewart but she did venture back as far as Ballymoney and was shown great kindness by the O'Kane family (the poultry merchants). When they heard about Anastasia's predicament, they allowed her to stay at their home and they looked after her and Guido until things started to progress. British Army Captain Jack Baxter, who was also Angelo's lawyer, was working on getting Anastasia back to Portstewart. Angelo also had connections through Charles Forte (of the Forte hotel empire), who used his influence with friends, in a political sense, in London to get Anastasia and Guido back to Portstewart. She eventually was allowed to return. When she did, she couldn't believe that her business was thriving. She got stuck in to running it again, extremely grateful for the generosity that had been shown to her by so many people in her absence.

The worst thing about this period of time for Anastasia was the unknown. She had no idea where her husband was or if he was safe. Neither did she have any idea where Nino and Corrado were. She prayed for their safety and she prayed that she would see them all again.

Nino, Maria Celeste
and Corrado, c.1940.

Nino and Corrado, c. 1939.

Anastasia and Guido, 1940.

Anastasia and Guido, c.1939.

Home Office No. M 10490.

Certificate No. **AZ** 12247

BRITISH NATIONALITY AND STATUS OF ALIENS ACT, 1914.

CERTIFICATE OF NATURALIZATION.

Whereas Pietro Morelli, known as Peter Morelli,

has applied to one of His Majesty's Principal Secretaries of State for a Certificate of Naturalization, alleging with respect to himself the particulars set out below, and has satisfied him that the conditions laid down in the above-mentioned Act for the grant of a Certificate of Naturalization are fulfilled in his case:

Now, therefore, in pursuance of the powers conferred on him by the said Act, the Secretary of State grants to the said

Pietro Morelli, known as Peter Morelli,

this Certificate of Naturalization, and declares that upon taking the Oath of Allegiance within the time and in the manner required by the regulations made in that behalf he shall, subject to the provisions of the said Act, be entitled to all political and other rights powers and privileges, and be subject to all obligations duties and liabilities, to which a natural-born British subject is entitled or subject, and have to all intents and purposes the status of a natural-born British subject.

In witness whereof I have hereto subscribed my name this 5th day of August, 1938.

HOME OFFICE,
LONDON.

Under Secretary of State.

PARTICULARS RELATING TO APPLICANT.

Full Name	Pietro MORELLI, known as Peter MORELLI.
Address	Stone Row, Coleraine, County Londonderry, N. Ireland.
Trade or occupation	Confectioner, Ice Cream Vendor and Supper Saloon Proprietor.
Place and date of birth	Casalattico, Italy. 29th April, 1885.
Nationality	Italian.
Single, married, etc.	Married.
Name of wife or husband	Annie Elizabeth.
Names and nationality of parents	Onorio and Clementina MORELLI. Italian.

(For Oath
see overleaf)

Oath of Allegiance.

...tro Morelli, known as Peter Morelli,

...ighty God that I will be faithful and bear true allegiance to His Majesty. ...the Sixth, His Heirs and Successors, according to law.

Pietro Morelli known as Peter Morelli

...subscribed this 27th day of August 1938, before me,

...tice of the Peace for H. for County Londonderry, N. Ireland

Commissioner for Oaths.

Unless otherwise indicated hereon, if the Oath of Allegiance is not taken ...one calendar month after the date of this Certificate, the Certificate shall ...ke effect.

Certificate of Naturalization.

No News is Good News

Nessuna Novita / Buone Novita

From Crumlin Road jail, Angelo had been taken to an internee camp in Bury, Lancashire where the conditions were very poor. He stayed in a disused, rat infested mill and began to feel extremely anxious about where he would be taken next. There were no signs, he just had to wait and see. Other internees began to assemble here from all over the United Kingdom. It quickly became apparent that this place was just a stopping gap and a point to assemble everybody for redirection. There was a lot of talk about Italians being sent to the Isle of Man or even abroad, but Angelo tried not to listen to hearsay and awaited his fate along with all the other enemy aliens. There were several thousand internees in Lancashire from Italy, Germany, France and even some Jewish people.

One day there seemed to be a lot of movement and officers began to assemble with what looked like lists of names. They were about to carry out a roll call. The commanding officer explained that if your name was called, you had to leave your group and move to the right. Angelo's name was called out and he dutifully moved to the right. This went on

for a while and at the end of the roll call, Angelo's name was called again and he was told to rejoin his original group. There had been some sort of mistake, but Angelo didn't argue and he did what he was told. The roll call had been used to differentiate between the '18B' category, that consisted of those who were considered to be more dangerous than their counterparts in the 'Fifth Column', which was what they called an 'ordinary' internee. So, originally Angelo had been picked to go with the 18B group. Some sort of guardian angel must have been looking down on him because group 18B, as it turned out, had a disastrous journey.

They had been picked to board a ship called the *Arandora Star,* a Blue Star liner that had previously been used as a pleasure cruiser. The internees learned that their destination aboard this ship would be St. Johns, Newfoundland. The *Arandora* set sail on 2 July 1940 from Liverpool. In all, she carried 1,673 people, made up of 174 officers and crew, 200 military guard, 479 German male internees, 86 German prisoners of war and 734 Italian male internees. As the ship reached the open sea, the conditions were good but as the ship steered west, it was suddenly torpedoed about 75 miles west of the Bloody Foreland in County Donegal.

The torpedo struck on the starboard at the after engine-room, which was flooded immediately to sea level. Two engineer officers and all the men below were either drowned or killed in the blast. The ship's turbines had been completely destroyed and the main emergency generators were also out of action. The ship was shrouded in darkness and all lines of communication were down. Luckily the ship's position had been recorded every half hour and as soon as the torpedo struck, the Chief Officer Mr Brown had sent the position to the wireless room with orders to send out an SOS. It was sent out and answered by Malin Head radio station. Out of a total of 12 boats, 10 were lowered and naturally, in the panic they were overcrowded by the swarms of people trying to clamber to safety. The list of the ship had rapidly increased and it became apparent that it was going to sink. Soon after, the *Arandora Star* rolled over, flung her bows vertically in the air and sank to the bottom of the ocean carrying many people with her. Left on the surface were the 10 lifeboats and hundreds of swimmers struggling in the oil slicked water. In this tragic disaster Captain EW Moulton and 12 other officers lost their lives, together with hundreds of internees. The total death toll was 805 souls. Today, this tragedy is marked by memorial plaques in Tuscany, Liverpool and Scotland. They pay tribute to the hundreds of internees who lost their lives on that fateful day.

Angelo was a very lucky man indeed. He never forgot what could have happened to him on that day and he thanked God that there had been a mistake in that roll call. Angelo's fate had been to travel to the Isle of Man. The island had also been used as a base for internees during WWI. The internees mainly settled in existing property, mostly in requisitioned boarding houses, which were cordoned off and used as a series of camps for the different nationalities. Most of the Italian internees had been sent to Peel or a section of the promenade in Douglas, which is where Angelo had been housed.

When Angelo had settled in Douglas, the lines of communication with Anastasia had re-opened. Internees were permitted one letter a week so he knew that she and Guido were safe and well, but the same could not be said for Nino and Corrado in Italy. There had been no communication and both Anastasia and Angelo had feared the worst. There had been no news at all. Desperately restless, they tried every way of obtaining some information and eventually Angelo learned that the boys had been evacuated from their home and had been taken to Calabria. However, that was all the news he was able to find out. Angelo felt so downhearted during this period. The unknown was almost worse than hearing bad news. He and Anastasia would have to wait for news and console themselves with the thought that no news was good news.

The Arandora Star.

Angelo Morelli just before his internment.

CHAPTER EIGHT

Internment

Internamento

Angelo spent just over three years on the Isle of Man. He had been placed in the 'Palace' camp, which was on the sea front. The boarding houses had been surrounded by barbed wire and had armed guards to ensure that the internees could not venture out onto the road or the promenade area. The houses were very close to the beach and in the good weather the internees would enjoy watching the comings and goings, especially the pretty girls. These boarding houses had been very well kept and were comfortable. Angelo had been placed in Grasmere Boarding House, the same house as some of his friends and acquaintances from Casalattico, including Lord Charles Forte. The men learned to make the most of their time together and forged strong bonds.

The men would pass their time by sitting in groups and talking of their different experiences of business, of war, of internment and of their families. They missed their families very much and each and every one of the men had good and bad days. They would read and sing, and with Angelo being so musical, he would take the lead with his beautiful Tenor voice. The men would sing Italian songs, some of which would make them feel very nostalgic. It was a little comfort for them being so far from home and Angelo greatly enjoyed these occasions.

The food was supplied by the government and it was bland. Rice, bread, kippers and potatoes was the staple diet, but as time progressed, the internees were allowed to accept food parcels from their loved ones and this was much better for Angelo, a great lover of Italian food. Naturally, as each person received their parcels, they consumed them themselves, often in rations so that they could make the food last as long as possible and mix it with the bland food for a bit of variety. Some of the men would hide their parcels or guard them with their lives. At one point, Anastasia had sent a rather large parcel to Angelo with his favourite foods and some Italian wine. When the parcel arrived it was just before Angelo's birthday on 21 October 1940. He decided that rather than keep the food for himself, he would share it with all the other men and create a party for his birthday. It was a gesture that all of the men appreciated. Amongst the internees were two Italian chefs who had been working at the Café Royal in London. They took the contents of the parcel and turned it into a beautiful

meal plus whatever else they could get their hands on and they were also permitted to consume the wine. So in one single night, they ate everything.

Angelo had always remembered this special night. His friends had drawn up a special menu, which showed their sense of humour and they had all signed it as a sort of makeshift birthday card. Angelo kept the menu as a memento of that day and as you can see, the signature of Lord Charles Forte is in the top left corner.

The situation was far from ideal, but after the initial upheaval of being taken from his home, Angelo and his fellow internees learned to live with it and they enjoyed themselves occasionally. In 2002, the BBC was planning to make a documentary about Angelo's life story. As part of that documentary, Angelo came back to Portstewart for a visit and he went to the Isle of Man to see all the familiar places of his internment. This trip evoked bitter sweet memories within him as he remembered a very different place all those years ago. Of course, the barbed wire had gone but the Grasmere Boarding House still stands. He also went to the Manx museum with his granddaughter Nicole to view the register of internees and recalled his roll number, 58733. What always struck me when talking to my Nonno about this time in his life was how openly and easily he talked about it and how, although he felt great guilt for what had happened, he accepted the situation and was gracious about it.

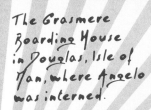

The Grasmere Boarding House in Douglas, Isle of Man, where Angelo was interned.

Group of 'Palace' camp internees, Angelo Morelli included, upon release in 1945.

Angelo's Birthday card with the signatures of the internees. The signature of Lord Charles Forte is included, as well as other surnames of the families that settled in Northern Ireland, including Cafolla, Rosato and Fusco.

Menu for Angelo's Birthday Party, 1940.

Menu Translation:

Morelli Starter

Spaghetti 'Internment Style'

The next line doesn't translate but it's a joke on the laxative effect of prunes.

Coffee

'Little wife's surprise'

CHAPTER NINE

Reunited
Finalmente Riuniti

After a painstakingly difficult period of waiting, news about Nino, Corrado and Maria Celeste's whereabouts began to filter through to Anastasia in Portstewart. Not only were they alive and well, but a series of twists and turns, and elements of profound luck meant that the Morelli family were on their way to being reunited again.

In Calabria, Maria had had an accident and had broken her hip. A family had taken her and her two grandsons in, given them extra food and looked after them well until such times that they could be moved again. Eventually, plans were made to move the family from Calabria. The Americans had organised for lorries to take everybody back to their homes, but on that journey, the closer they got to Casino, it was beginning to look like it was too dangerous to continue the journey. There were still bombs lying about and then the lorry carrying the boys got a puncture and had to stop in Casino. Nino and Corrado have never forgotten the dreadful sight that the saw there. Bodies were lying on the roads and scavengers were having a field day amongst them, pilfering their belongings such as jewellery and searching their pockets for anything of value. The Allied victory at Casino meant that they could return home and they were close at this stage of doing just that, but not close enough it seemed.

It was simply not going to be possible to get through Casino, the dangers were too great, so the Germans had to rethink quickly and they re-routed the lorry to Aversa, which is very close to Naples. Here the boys and their grandmother were placed in kind of penitentiary camp which had been used to treat people with mental problems. The boys stayed there for a further three months and thought that they would never get to see their parents again. Anastasia and Angelo were becoming increasingly concerned that the boys would not be able to get back to Casalattico. However, the Morelli guardian angel was about to come up trumps again. As they waited in Aversa for news of another move, Nino and Corrado had been sent for by the commander of the camp. They wondered what he could possibly want with them? Perhaps he had a job for them or they were about to get in to trouble!

The commander of the camp was called William Irwin Cunningham (or WIC) who had previously been the town clerk of Portstewart. He had been posted in Italy for the duration of the hostilities. He had been looking through the names on his register when suddenly he came across a very familiar surname. He wondered if Nino and Corrado could be related to Angelo Morelli. He asked them about their family and the boys confirmed that Angelo was indeed their father and they told him of their difficulties getting back to Casalattico. WIC told them not to worry and he would make the necessary arrangements for Nino and Corrado to get back home to Portstewart. The boys were absolutely ecstatic, who could imagine that thousands of miles from Portstewart, a local man would find them and show such kindness? Nonno has always described this moment as a 'miracle' and that is exactly what it was.

WIC made arrangements with the British authorities for the boys to be repatriated so they could return to Portstewart straight away, but first they were permitted to go back to Casalattico to collect their belongings. Upon arriving there, they discovered that there was nothing there. The house had been completely cleaned out. Help was on the horizon once again when another gentleman from Portstewart, Colonel Frizzell, who was stationed in Rome, offered his assistance. Anastasia was very good friends with his wife and she said that she would give Anastasia some coupons to buy clothes

for them. Anastasia had saved some coupons also and they put them together and bought some clothes for the two boys and their grandmother. Mrs Frizzell sent the parcels to Italy via her husband in Rome and he arranged for a soldier to drive all the way from Rome to San Andrea in a jeep to deliver the clothes.

Angelo too was granted release from the Isle of Man at this time, but his release had conditions. He had been asked to carry out 'work of national importance' and didn't have much choice but to accept. He was sent to North Wales to help in the war effort, working for the Navy and Royal Air Force who were fighting against Germany and Japan. Eventually though, through the intervention of friends, Angelo was permitted to return to Portstewart to be with Anastasia and Guido.

Nino and Corrado stayed in San Andrea with their grandmother and waited for news from WIC about their onward journey. Maria Celeste, once settled, had decided that she would stay in Casalattico. She was very keen to get back to some sort of normality after all the upheaval, and wanted to sort the house out and make it look like a home again. Eventually, a telegram arrived with news that train tickets had been bought and arrangements made for the two boys to travel back to Northern Ireland. The boys were accompanied on that journey by a family friend called Fiore Salvetta, who had also been stationed in Italy. He was travelling back to Dublin. Nino and Corrado travelled with Fiore as far as Dover where they were met by their uncle Mario who had a business in Broadstairs. The boys felt happy to be with family again and Anastasia and Angelo were delighted that in a few short days their family would be together again. Mario arranged for the boys to fly back to Belfast. That was a big thing then and the boys were so excited to be going back home. The plane touched down, ironically, on the Isle of Man before the final leg of the journey to Belfast.

Anastasia, Angelo and Guido were waiting at Short Brothers Harbour Airport to welcome them back. After four long years, in 1945, the Morelli family would be together again at last. Nino and Corrado couldn't contain their excitement and when they stepped onto the tarmac in Belfast, they had an emotional reunion with their parents and younger brother. This is a moment that the three brothers remember with great fondness. Nino and Corrado looked a lot different to their brother Guido. Nino was now fourteen years old and weighed just six stone. It was apparent that food had been scarce. Guido was visually more robust and they all had a good laugh at each other. Guido hadn't really had the chance to know his two brothers before they got separated and he found it very strange having to share his mother again. The boys bonded though and developed a very strong relationship with each other that still remains to this day. Nino and Corrado could speak hardly any English and it took time for them to learn the language again. Naturally, the boys were treated very well on their return by family and friends because of what they had gone through.

William Irwin Cunningham

Angela and Anastasia reunited after internment, c. 1945.

Brothers reunited,
Portstewart 1945. From left
to right: Nino, Corrado and
Guido.

A family again. From left to right: Corrado, Angelo, Nino,
Anastasia and Guido.

CHAPTER TEN

The Family Business
Affari di Famiglia

In the post war years, the economy became stronger and the family business began to prosper. Times were good, but the hours were long and the work was hard, so Anastasia was pleased to have a little more help. Nino, Corrado and Guido all helped their parents in the shop during the summer and at weekends.

Corrado and Guido went to Terenure College in Dublin for a year before returning to the North Coast. Nino finished his education locally at Coleraine Academical Institution. The boys had missed quite a bit of school so they were a lot older than the others in their class and found it difficult to fit in. Corrado in particular found it difficult to catch up and wasn't interested in school. He developed an intense passion for motor cars, which perhaps started when Angelo bought his first car, and would bunk off school and go to Belfast to the model shop.

After finishing their education, all three boys decided to join their parents in the family business. It wasn't a pre-determined decision for them, as they were never forced into it by their parents. They genuinely had a passion for it and wanted to help it expand and develop into something fantastic. Peter Morelli was still in business also. Sadly, his wife Annie Dymond had passed away but he met and married another woman named Margherita Offredi. She was Italian, although lived in Hastings, and they had been introduced by an aunt. Margherita or Aunty Margaret, as she was affectionately known, was a lovely, gentle person. Peter wanted to retire, so Angelo took over the shop in Stone Row, Coleraine and another shop in Portrush that Peter had acquired called the 'Shamrock Corner'. This shop would later become known as the 'Savoy'. So, as the business expanded, Angelo and Anastasia had decided that the three shops would be their legacy to each of their boys.

The boys all grew up in the family business and it was an environment in which they all felt very comfortable. They each had their own roles and responsibilities, and worked hard. Corrado made the ice cream, Nino would work in a trailer which was sited outside the Savoy in Portrush and Guido would do a little of everything in each of the shops. They would all muck in wherever they were needed. Corrado's passion for cars and motor sports developed greatly, and he would work on go carts in his spare time and competed in races locally. Nino's love was golf and he spent every spare moment on the golf course. Guido's passion was for swimming and diving, and he could often be found diving in the Crescent in Portstewart. Guido and Corrado also inherited their father's musical talents. Guido played guitar and sang in a local skiffle group called the 'Bann Valley Ramblers', and Corrado has a beautiful singing voice. They didn't get much spare time, but when they did, they indulged in their passions. This of course was all before they developed an interest in girls.

Angelo and Anastasia were very much still in charge of the business, and at times they could be quite strict with their sons. However, the boys all found ways to get around this. They would cover for each other, which usually meant telling a lot of white lies to get an extra hour on the golf course or a quick spin in a car. The boys enjoyed it when Angelo and Anastasia would go back to Italy for holidays, as this gave them a little more of a free rein on things. I've heard many stories, but none of which my father or his brothers are prepared to confirm or deny. It's always good fun guessing though!

In the late 1950s, Angelo and Anastasia decided to make some changes to the shop in Portstewart. They expanded it to create two separate shops, and so, in 1958, the 'Sundae Garden' was born. This was perhaps the most iconic Morelli outlet of all. It certainly is the most talked about and remembered. It was ahead of its time design-wise with its art-deco features, famous sunflower tables and three legged chairs, which are still in existence (if a little bruised and battered). Angelo was always a man for firsts. He imported the first 'Gaggia' espresso coffee machine into Ireland, which sat pride of place in the Sundae Garden. It was his baby and he was very proud of it. He was probably serving up Cappuccinos before anyone even knew what they were. In the early 1960s, Angelo also acquired the property beside the Sundae Garden and made his shop bigger.

The late 50s and early 60s were an extremely busy time, as the family also opened a new shop in The Diamond in Coleraine. It too was ahead of its time and as you can see from the picture the focus was also on the art-deco styling. The shop featured a 'star' ceiling, Formica flooring and bold interior design. Again, this shop is still often talked about. It was hugely popular, especially with other local business people from the area. Branded crockery, espresso cups and ashtrays are still in existence from this era. Back in those days, attention to detail was the key to anything Angelo and Anastasia did. This they had that down to a fine art. The 'Italian' influence probably had a lot to do with the styling of the shops. Angelo had kept strong alliances and friendships in Italy and was therefore able to import the latest catering equipment quite easily.

No visit to the North Coast was complete without a visit to a Morelli establishment whether it was for fish and chips, an ice cream soda, a real Italian coffee or indeed the most indulgent thing on offer, a knickerbocker glory. There is no doubt at all that Anastasia was solely responsible for the success of the business at this stage. She became an extremely shrewd business woman in the absence of her husband during the war, laying the foundations and they were solid ones. She worked tirelessly to make each and every aspect of her business work, and she instilled that work ethic into her sons. Never a person to take anything for granted, she quietly worked in the background, taking very little time for herself. She was a great believer in the phrase 'charity begins at home' and also a woman of great faith. She believed in giving and every year, at Easter, she would donate a day's takings to the church. I like to say that my Nonna was the original crusader for 'Girlpower'.

Guido, Corrado and
Nino working, c.1955.

Peter Morelli, Margaret Oresti (Morelli)
and Angelo.

Corrado in his ice cream
making uniform, pictured in
Portrush, c.1952.

Nino, c.1956.

Corrado go cart racing in Portrush, c.1958.

Nino in the Morelli's trailer in
Portrush.

Guido performing with his
skiffle group, c.1958.

Angelo with his beloved 'Gaggia' coffee machine, Portstewart, 1958.

Anastasia behind the counter in The Lido, c.1960.

Interior of Morelli's, The Diamond, Coleraine.

All hands on deck in the Sundae Garden, 1958.

The interior of the sundae garden, with its famous sunflower tables and three legged chairs.

CHAPTER ELEVEN

Brides for the Brothers
Spose per Fratelli

Nino, Corrado and Guido were now at an age where they were becoming interested in courting girls. Angelo had always made his sons aware that he wanted them to marry Italian girls. Whilst they understood his wishes, it was quite difficult to meet Italian girls on the North Coast, so they began courting the locals and had a lot of fun. They would socialise at all the popular places of that era. Barry's, the Arcadia, the Boat House in Coleraine and anywhere where they could let their hair down after a busy day's work.

Nino began courting Nan McAleese from Portrush and things were beginning to get serious. They announced their engagement and were married in 1956. They took over the shop in The Diamond in Coleraine.

Corrado courted Elizabeth Mercer, who was a first cousin of Nino's wife Nan. Their courtship didn't come without its problems. Elizabeth's father didn't approve of their relationship. Corrado recalls taking Elizabeth out on a date and calling for her. As they drove away, Elizabeth's father chased them down the road on his bicycle, but Corrado persevered and

managed to convince her father that he was good enough for his daughter. They were married in 1958 and took over the Savoy café in Portrush.

Guido met Rosemarie Williams in Portrush. She lived in Dublin, but she was half Italian. Her mother was a DiVito and Rosemarie came to Portrush to help in her Uncle's shop 'DiVito's' for the summer. Guido fell in love with her and they had a long courtship, with Guido often travelling to Dublin to visit her. They were married in Dublin in 1961. They ran another shop in Portstewart called the 'Sunset Grill'.

Laughably, even after the boys had become engaged to their respective wives, Angelo took them to Italy in the vain hope that they would meet Italian wives. This was Angelo's last ditch effort to make them see sense, but the boys let this go over their heads. They had all made their choices and wanted to marry to the women they had fallen in love with back home.

It took the girls some time to get used to married life in a big traditional Italian family. Rosemarie perhaps had a better idea of what she was getting into having come from an Italian family herself, but it was a little more of a challenge for Nan and Elizabeth. Anastasia taught them how to cook 'Italian-style' and they all had to learn about the business pretty quickly. But they had good teachers, picked things up very rapidly and easily, and soon got into the swing of it.

The brothers and their new wives all got on very well. They had great fun socialising together and going to family functions, as well as getting to know the members of the extended family. They took holidays together and went to Italian dances, where members of the Italian community in Ireland, North and South would all get together and socialise. These Italian dances still take place today. Seeing how well the three couples got on, Angelo made a suggestion to form a company. The boys thought about his suggestion, but Corrado decided against it. He thought that as they all got on so well, he didn't want to jeopardise that relationship and wanted to keep things as they were. That was a decision he didn't live to regret. It proved much better for everybody to remain independent in their businesses, as it avoided fighting and disagreements.

Before long the news came that Nino and Nan were expecting their first child. A girl, Angelo and Anastasia's first grandchild, was born in May 1958. They named her Rossana. She's affectionately known as 'Elderberry' by all of her cousins as she is the eldest. Incidentally, I'm the youngest.

Nino and Nan's wedding, 1956.

Courting days. From left to right:
Nino, Nan, Elizabeth and Corrado.

Corrado and Elizabeth's
wedding, 1958.

Guido and Rosemarie's wedding, 1961.

Sisters in law united.

Morelli's at The Diamond in Coleraine.

The Sunset Grill in Portrush.

The Savoy café in Portrush.

CHAPTER TWELVE

The Family Grows
La Famiglia Cresce

After Rossana was born, grandchildren kept arriving and the family began to expand. Nino and Nan had four children, Rossana, Angelo, Damian and Nicole. Corrado and Elizabeth also had four, Aldo, Lisa, Piera and Dino. Guido and Rosemarie had five, Marino, Romeo, Tania, Arnaldo and I.

As you can see, the Italian family traditions have all been kept going in our names, and even the great grandchildren all have Italian names. Today the Morelli family consists of thirteen grandchildren and nineteen great grandchildren of Angelo and Anastasia. When you take spouses into account, the family reaches close to fifty members. As you can imagine, family occasions can be a little overwhelming, especially for newcomers. However, one thing I can say is, we are all very close. Cousins are friends and social occasions are plentiful so we see a lot of each other socially as well as in business.

Naturally, as the family began to grow, there had to be changes. Corrado decided to change his business a little in the early 70s and swapped the catering industry for the amusement business. In 1973, he opened 'Kiddieland', an outdoor amusement arcade with some children's rides and an indoor gaming machine area. He bought the house beside the business premises, called 'West Strand House' as it overlooked the West Strand beach in Portrush. This business was successful for him and he expanded further in 1975 when he took over premises on the main street in Portrush and opened a second amusements called 'Sportsland'. At this stage Guido and Rosemarie had taken over the Savoy café in Portrush and lived above it. This is where I grew up.

The Savoy was at the corner of Eglinton Street and was and still is known by the locals as 'Morelli's Corner'. I have the fondest memories of working in this shop as a child. My father gave me my first role in the business when I was nine. My job was to pour the minerals from the coke machine for the food orders. I couldn't reach the machine, so I stood on a crate. When I was tall enough to see over the counter, I would serve the customers take away ice cream at the kiosk at the front of the shop. As I got a bit older I was promoted to clearing tables and washing dishes, but I didn't really like that! I wanted to serve the customers and talk to people, so I went back to the kiosk and have vivid memories of hanging out the window, much to my father's despair. My first packet of wages contained £6.00 and I thought I was just great. My brothers and sisters all worked in the Savoy too, so it was quite normal.

Nino and Nan and their family eventually took over the Sundae Garden in Portstewart. This shop also had living accommodation above, so they converted it a little and my cousins also grew up very much involved in the business. As my cousins and I got older, the family began to splinter off in different directions. My cousin Angelo immigrated to Australia and became a social worker. He stayed there for many years, but has since returned and has opened 'Morelli's 22' in Church Street, Coleraine. Corrado's youngest son Dino inherited his father's passion for motor sports and became very successful, making it to formula 3000. A rather bad accident hampered his efforts though, and he now owns 'Morelli's Pizzeria Napoletana', an authentic Italian pizzeria on Belfast's Lisburn Road. Corrado's eldest son Aldo's business is Bingo. In all, there are

now twelve separate Morelli enterprises including 'Morelli's' restaurant' in Puerto Banus, Spain, which is run by Aldo's son Silvano. I guess you could say that we have all inherited our Nonno and Nonna's entrepreneurial spirit and I don't think any of us would have it any other way.

The business over the years has not been without its troubles. Corrado's business 'Sportsland' was destroyed in 1976 in an IRA bomb, just a year after he opened. This was a major set back but he was eventually able to rebuild the amusements and he re-opened again in 1978.

The flagship 'Morelli's' has always been in Portstewart and I think it's for this particular shop that the Morelli family will always be remembered. It's difficult to believe that it all began in a small shop run by just one man. It has changed greatly over the years, but as with everything, moving with the times is what you've got to do to stay in business. The shop itself on the promenade has had many revamps and facelifts over the years, but as you can see from the photographs, it has never lost its presence.

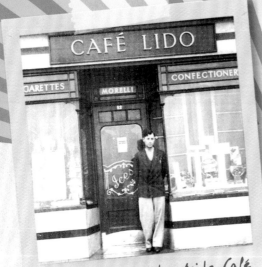

Angelo pictured outside Café Lido, Portstewart, c. 1930.

Morelli's, the Promenade, Portstewart, 1970s.

Morelli's, the Promenade, Portstewart, 1990s.

Morelli's, the Promenade, Portstewart, 1980s.

Sportsland amusements in Portrush.

The Morelli family 2003, pictured at the Royal Court during a family reunion.

Dino the racer.

Four generations. From left to right: Angelo, Nino Junior, Damian and Nino.

CHAPTER THIRTEEN

Back to the Motherland
Ritorno in Patria

Angelo and Anastasia were drawing close to retirement age by the early 70s and they had thought about this time a lot. They had always said that when they did retire, they would go back to Italy because that's where their roots belonged. In 1974 they travelled back to their native land to enjoy the fruits of their labour and retire from working life. They kept a small flat in Portstewart so that they could return as often as they liked.

Angelo, as an only child, had obviously inherited his parent's home in San Andrea. The house had been built in the 1920s and needed modernisation, so Anastasia and Angelo made improvements to it over time. They had of course been back and forward to Italy in between times, but now that they were there more permanently, they could spend time doing the small, cosmetic improvements that they wanted to do. They also greatly enjoyed spending time with their old friends and family that had also returned to Casalattico in later life. Nonna was a fantastic crotchetier and would spend hours making various things for her daughters in law and her friends, such as cushion covers. She even took

on projects as large as complete bedding covers. It was amazing watching her at work; the needle would go so quickly that you could barely see it and she could have a full conversation with you whilst crocheting at the same time.

Angelo had set about developing the land beside his house into two villas for Nino and Corrado so that when they wanted to return to Italy, they each had their own homes for their family. This project took a lot of time to complete, but Angelo took it on with gusto and two beautiful homes were completed and ready to be enjoyed. Nonno wanted so much for his family to remain true to their Italian roots and he would do all that he could to encourage you to go there for a holiday and of course we did. My cousins and I all love going back to Italy. It's so peaceful and full of culture, and a great place to totally switch off. I remember one particular Christmas, when I was about two years old, my father and his brothers decided that we would all have a family Christmas in Italy. We set off in the car, and being in my 'terrible twos' period, Santa had to come to the car with my toys as I just wouldn't be quiet.

I remember my Fisher Price Post Office well, and so do my brothers and sister because I wouldn't give them any peace to read or sleep until they played with me and posted their Christmas cards. I think my poor father Guido vowed never to take me on a long car journey again after that trip.

Nonno and Nonna would travel back to Portstewart for special occasions such as christenings, weddings and their own special wedding anniversaries so that the whole family could celebrate together. They loved these times when the whole family were together and I remember them coming back and forth quite often when I was a child.

Nonno had taken a keen interest in local politics and he became Deputy Mayor of Casalattico for many years. He was instrumental in making improvements to the area, especially when an earthquake hit in the 1980s, which caused extensive damage to some of the properties in the local and surrounding areas. New roofs were required for most dwellings in San Andrea and Nonno dealt with the authorities in Rome and secured the funding for the necessary repair work to be carried out. Thankfully there have been no major earthquakes since, but tremors still occur quite often as it lies on a fault line.

Nonno also took on a project in his later life that was very dear to his own heart. There is a small church in San Andrea named 'Madonna Degli Angeli' and it was in a terrible state of repair. Angelo thought that since San Andrea didn't have its own church, he would set about improving it and returning it to its former glory. Nonno took on this job and put every effort into it. He wrote to everyone he knew in the entire area, no matter where they were in the world, and asked for donations big or small to help with this project. He came back to Ireland and visited the people he had written to and collected as much as he could to make the necessary repairs. This was perhaps the biggest achievement, after business accomplishments, that Angelo had made in his life. When the Church was completed, he was extremely proud of it. He would delight in giving tours round his little church to any visitors to Casalattico, and knew off by heart where everything had come from and who had paid for what. He even named the pews in the small church after the people who had made donations. The church wasn't used for a weekly service, but instead for special masses particular to San Andrea.

Casalattico.

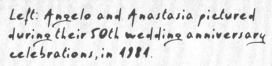

Left: Angelo and Anastasia pictured during their 50th wedding anniversary celebrations, in 1981.

Above: The Morelli family at the anniversary party.

Visiting Lord Charles. From left to right: Rosemarie, Anastasia, Lord Charles Forte, Lady Irene Forte, Angelo, Nino and Nan.

The Comino Valley, showing the village of San Andrea.

CHAPTER FOURTEEN

All Change
Tutto Cambia

The late 1990s saw the beginning of extensive changes in the Morelli family business. My brother Arnaldo had completed a degree in Business at Cardiff University and it was his desire to create a different angle to the business. He saw the potential to wholesale Morelli's ice cream to distributors, retailers, hotels, restaurants and convenience stores all over Ireland. We already had a small production facility at the back of Savoy café in Portrush and ice cream had been manufactured there for many years to service our own outlets in Portrush and to supply a few local customers. The Portstewart shop had a small production plant at the back of the shop so they were able to service their own needs.

The wholesale business was established in 1997 and it started off in a small way. Arnaldo secured several new retail customers and set up a 'Scoop' concept where a customer would invest in a small ice cream display cabinet and we would provide them with stock and training. A weekly delivery schedule was set up to service different areas of the province on a weekly basis. Business improved year on year

and in 2006 the factory moved to a new purpose-built production facility at Sperrin Business Park in Coleraine.

Big changes were also afoot for Portstewart. Plans had been made for a full refurbishment of the whole premises. This would be a full turnkey project and the family commissioned an Italian company called Arredogel to complete the project. The family wanted to bring the site into the new century and working closely with the architects, that was exactly what they did. The plans were drawn up and agreed upon. Before long, the work had started and it was an exciting time for the business. However, this project did not come without its problems. When preparations were being made to close the shop down for the refurbishment, a fire destroyed the whole site. Luckily, most items of value had already been moved and the damage, although extensive to the building, did not cause as much chaos as it would have done if circumstances had been different.

The changes to the landmark shop in Portstewart were completed in 2002 and it was impressive. The property had been converted to one bigger shop with a brand new look. The décor was contemporary with a light coloured marble floor, a sweeping counter area, glass back bar, an extensive seating area and new purpose built kitchen, preparation and storage facilities. A far cry from the Old Café Lido of the 1930s. All that remained at this stage was to gain Angelo's seal of approval. He came back from Italy to see the changes for himself, and he was delighted with the end results. The official opening took place and Angelo of course cut the ribbon. He told his guests about the times of the Ice palace and recalled how different business had been back then.

That same year, Angelo Morelli's story caught the interest of a producer from the BBC and they came up with the idea of making a documentary. Angelo was excited by this and immediately agreed. My Nonno loved to talk to others about his experiences, so the daunting task of being interviewed for many hours in front of a camera didn't phase him. A small camera crew travelled to the family home in Italy and interviewed Nonno for many hours about his life and the history of the family. This documentary evoked a lot of emotion within him and we as a family even learned things about his experiences that were not previously discussed or known. A reunion was organised as part of the documentary. We managed to get the whole family together at the Royal Court Hotel in Portrush, which made Nonno very happy. It isn't often that the whole family gets together and in this case everyone had made the effort to be there, with my cousin Angelo even travelling home from Australia. It was a great occasion and Nonno made a speech telling us that he was proud of all of us and that it had been his wish for a day like this to be arranged before his 'final days'. We all remember this day with very fond memories. The documentary was completed and screened on BBC 1 Northern Ireland in September 2003. I can remember that day quite clearly. We gathered to watch it in Portstewart and were all naturally a bit nervous but there really wasn't any need. It portrayed the story of my grandparents admirably and we were all a bit emotional as parts of it were very poignant and touchingly personal.

The Morelli's Ice Cream Factory.

Angelo opening the new look Morelli's in Portstewart, in 2002.

The new look interior of Morelli's Portstewart.

Angelo Morelli, 2003.

CHAPTER FIFTEEN

We are Family

Famiglia Unita

We lost our Nonna Anastasia in 1994 after a long illness. I was only fourteen, and although I hadn't really had a chance in my lifetime to know her as well as I would have liked, she will always remain in my heart as the woman whose kindness not only touched me, but everyone she met. People still tell me stories about her to this day. She was a unique woman who had such aplomb in her family. She had a very fitting send off in Casalattico and was laid to rest in her home village. Angelo missed her dreadfully and after her death he would spend longer periods of time in Portstewart with the rest of the family.

Nonno Angelo passed away on Valentines Day 2007. As he was one of Northern Ireland's original ice cream men, it was somewhat appropriate that he died at the age of '99'. He had a short illness but had been independent right up to his 99th year. Most members of the family travelled to Italy for his funeral and if he was looking down on that day, I know he would have been very happy with the whole family getting together for his very fitting and memorable send off.

Nonno and Nonna had a desire for their grandchildren and great grandchildren to know their roots and were adamant that they did not want our links to Italy to diminish after they were gone. As the region in Italy is quite rural, there isn't much to do for young kids. If you want to go to the beach, you have to drive further to the coast or to the local water park. However, Angelo in his wisdom had come up with a plan to keep us coming back there. He made plans to create a swimming pool at the back of his house so that we could go there and enjoy a family holiday. I have to say that his cunning plan has worked. Most of us go back to holiday in Italy at least once a year and will continue to do so for a long time to come.

The Morelli brand has expanded greatly since the deaths of Nonno and Nonna, and with each positive change and success that is achieved within the business, our thoughts always turn to them. The wholesale side of the business has made great headway in recent years, having secured a contract to supply Tesco Northern Ireland stores with ice cream in two of the most popular flavours, double cream vanilla and honeycomb. Morelli franchises have also been created in Letterkenny (County Donegal), Belfast (County Antrim), Newcastle (County Down) and Ballyhalbert (County Down).

Guido (my father) is still very much involved in the business, although he claims to be retired! His talent and vision is an inspiration to us all and when it comes to developing new flavours and recipe formulations, he is always tireless in his quest for perfection, often repeating his mantra "sometimes you have to take a couple of steps back before you can move forward." His latest recipe is a 'sugar free' dairy ice cream. He worked on this recipe for a long time, tinkering with different ingredients until he reached a formulation that he was happy with. The inspiration behind this came from him being diagnosed with diabetes a few years ago. Being an ice cream lover, he didn't think it was fair for him not to be able to enjoy ice cream guilt free, and so he created a fantastic recipe and has since improved it even further. He named it 'Senza'. The Italian translation is 'Without'.

The Morelli ice cream factory currently produces all of the ice cream for our family owned stores and franchises, as well as over eighty wholesale customers based across Ireland. The production process has changed greatly since the days when Uncle Peter accompanied the block of ice on the tram to freeze the ice cream. These days we have modern machinery which enables us to freeze the product pretty quickly. In Nonno's ice cream making days, the flavours were very limited also. Vanilla was always the best seller and eventually more flavours were introduced like Strawberry and Chocolate. Now we have a selection of over forty flavours available all the time. We like to keep things fresh by introducing new flavours to our offering every single year. For this year, Guido has developed a new 'Luxury Double Chocolate', 'Very Berry Cheesecake' and 'Eton Mess'. I have to admit, the best part of my job comes just before Easter every year when we are deciding upon the new flavours. This year was difficult. After sampling over twenty potential new flavours, we eventually narrowed it down to five. Numerous tasting meetings took place with the extended family and we rated each one individually. The ones with the highest scores made the cut! A serious business indeed!

The ingredients are a hugely important part of making Morelli's ice cream. The 'original' recipe is still in use today, although developed for use with more advanced machinery and production methods. We produce a Dairy Vanilla recipe which is used for all of our vanilla-based flavours. We also produce a non-dairy recipe, a chocolate recipe and the 'Senza' sugar free recipe. The question I'm most often asked is, "Is there really a secret ingredient?" The answer is yes, but it's so secret that even I don't know what it is! We source our flavours from the famously innovative Italian flavour houses that specialise in the art of Gelato or ice cream. That coupled with Irish Double Cream creates the creamy luxurious texture. Additional ingredients include pure Sicilian Pistachio nuts, rum soaked raisins, the finest Belgian chocolate and real fruit pulps. Northern Irish people really do have a sweet tooth. This became evident when our best selling flavour shifted over recent years from Vanilla to Honeycomb.

Although tastes have changed over the years, surprisingly, it's still the traditional ice cream treats that remain the most popular. Knickerbocker Glory's, Sliders, Nougat Wafers and Oyster Shells still remain flavour of the day, especially on the North Coast, and yes, people still ask for a 'poke'. European influences have created a more discerning palate, but I think the old favourites will remain for many years to come.

Morelli's Belgian Chocolate Ice Cream pictured in one of the original shell ice cream dishes from the Sundae Garden.

Leila (my niece) enjoying a Morelli's ice cream.

Advertisement for Senza sugar free ice cream.

Simon Moore (Tesco) and Arnaldo Morelli promoting the availability of Morelli's Ice Cream in Tesco Northern Ireland.

Ice Cream Friends
Amici Gelatieri

The Ice Cream Alliance is a trade organisation that represents Ice Cream Manufacturers in the UK and Ireland. The Alliance is made up of geographical divisions throughout the UK. In the early 1990s, the President of the Alliance at the time, Michael Minchella, came over to Northern Ireland to meet with manufacturers based here and to encourage them to become more involved in the Ice Cream Alliance. At this time Northern Ireland was not represented on the board of directors. As time went on, a great friendship had been formed between Michael and my father Guido. Michael encouraged him to represent Northern Ireland on the board and Guido went along to the head office in Nottingham where he met like-minded people who were all passionate about ice cream.

We have been members of the Alliance for many years, attended their exhibitions and entered the famous National Ice Cream Competitions. Guido sat on the board for five years and was proud to be elected as President in 1995. Arnaldo (my brother) followed in his footsteps and also sat on the board. He became the youngest ever President of the

alliance in 2005, aged just 29. I too became involved in the ICA, but not on the board. I write articles in the members magazine, naturally called Ice Cream magazine. This role gives me great enjoyment and a chance to meet the many colourful characters in the industry.

The Ice Cream Alliance is a very special association. It may be based on business and industry but firm friendships have also been forged. The ice cream industry is a truly unique one. I have never met a group of people who are more passionate about the product they make. Problems are shared, laughs are had, triumphs in competition are celebrated amongst everybody and new things are learned every year at the annual exhibition. There are many Italian families in the Alliance who all started out in a similar way to us. Having this in common creates a unique bond and when we get together every year in Harrogate, it's more like old friends getting together than a business event.

The Ice Cream Alliance competitions create a 'buzz' within the industry every year. The much coveted Silver challenge Cups are what everybody dreams of bringing home. Ice Cream is entered into several different classes and they are judged by a panel of experts, some of whom have been in the ice cream business for several decades. It's tough putting your ice cream up against the cream of the crop in the whole country, but the feeling of winning a cup is truly overwhelming.

We have had several successes in the Ice Cream competitions in recent years. In 2006/2007, Morelli's Ice Cream created history in the Ice Cream Alliance when we won first prize in two vanilla classes, the first company to secure the coveted 'double'. We went on to win another first prize for vanilla in 2009. It's particularly difficult to win a vanilla class as they always attract the most entries. This is an achievement of which we are extremely proud.

The highlight of the ice cream calendar is the Ice Cream Ball, which also takes place in Harrogate. This is a chance for the whole industry to get together and celebrate the successes stories of the competitions as well as to enjoy the social aspect of the exhibition.

Another important ice cream event is the annual SIGEP (*Salone Internazionale Gelateria, Pasticceria e Panificazione Artigianali*) exhibition, which takes place in the Italian seaside town of Rimini. This is the largest dedicated ice cream, chocolate and patisserie exhibition in the World. The event takes place over several days and it's always a hugely enjoyable experience.

(Left) Guido Morelli making a sundae as President of the Ice Cream Alliance, in Blackpool, 1996.

Ice Cream Alliance logo.

(Above) Arnaldo Morelli pulling some 'pokes' as President of the Ice Cream Alliance, in Harrogate, 2006.

(Left) The National Executive Council of the Ice Cream Alliance, 1992.

Arnaldo, Daniela, Guido and Marino pictured in Harrogate, in 2009, with the first prize Silver Challenge cup for dairy Artisan vanilla.

Ice Cream Friends, 2009.

From left to right, Front:
Peter Giacopazzi, Marino Morelli, Guido Morelli, Michael Minchella and Joe Minchella.

Back:
Fillipo Mancini, Rick Hewitt, Arnaldo Morelli, David Otterburn, David Egui, Joesf Boni, Daniela Morelli, Mark Mancini and Alasdair Dobson.

CHAPTER SEVENTEEN

One Hundred Years

Cento Anni

I can't quite believe that our family business is One Hundred years old. And although I have only been around for thirty of them, I could see right from the beginning of my life that the family business was special. My Nonna and Nonno were extremely determined to succeed in business and their work ethic has been instilled in each and every member of the Morelli family. It was their wish that the future generations of the family would never forget their roots and I don't think any of us could forget for one second the humble beginnings of that business.

As a family we have splintered off in different directions over the years as all families do. Each section of the family runs their own businesses, all still baring the Morelli name. Four or five years ago, we knew that we were getting close to our centenary year and had a general sort of discussion about how we were going to celebrate. We all agreed that we would have some sort of party to mark the occasion.

In February 2010, we arranged a family meeting to discuss the event in more detail. A group of about twelve of us gathered at Morelli's in Portstewart and we discussed our different ideas. Eventually,

we reached a decision. We wanted to create a party for everyone, especially our customers. It stared as a simple idea, but it has now escalated to a full programme of events that will take place throughout 2011.

A photographic exhibition at Flowerfield Arts Centre in Portstewart will begin the celebrations, opening on 1 July and continuing for the whole month. A selection of historical photographs will chart the story of Morelli's. It will illustrate the business from its beginnings in Stone Row right up to the present day. Many of the pictures have come from Angelo's own collection and this event is sure to evoke many memories among the residents of the Triangle area.

Our second series of events will take place on 23 July. We have taken on the daunting task of attempting a Guinness World Record. During this record we shall be trying to create the "longest chain of people licking ice cream simultaneously". The record was set in April 2010, in Augustana USA and in order to beat it, we need over 2,700 people to take part. We are aiming to thrash the current record and are hoping to attract 3,200 participants to the

Dominican College in Portstewart on the day. Later that same evening, there will be live music from an Italian band, a laser light display, an authentic Italian Opera singer and lots of other surprises. So as you can see, what started out as a small idea, has turned into something spectacular. Our mission is to create a fun event that our customers and friends will remember for many years to come.

The 29 September will see the first annual Morelli's Centenary Golf Tournament take place at Portstewart Golf Club. The winner will take home the specially commissioned 'Morelli Centenary Cup' which will, with a bit of luck become a tradition and be played for around the same time annually in Portstewart.

Last but not least, we have planned the 'Morelli Centenary Ball' for 30 September, which will round off the season of events. Portstewart Golf Club will host 180 guests, made up of family, friends, customers, suppliers and peers, all gathering for a formal celebration to mark our Centenary year. The sub-committee are busy organising this affair with military precision. The only thing left to work out is who gets to cut the cake!

From that initial planning meeting in February 2010, we are now hammering out the final details at our fifteenth meeting. Guido, Nino and Corrado have attended nearly all the meetings alongside their families. We have enjoyed this time immensely and working so closely on this project has indeed brought us closer together as a family. Amazingly,

there has not been one single fight or disagreement throughout the planning stages. Perhaps we are mellowing with age! We have also decided to support NICHS (Northern Ireland Chest Heart & Stroke) throughout all of our planned events. This is a charity that is particularly close to our hearts, having lost both my mother and our aunty Nan to heart disease in 2001 and 2009 respectively. They too were a huge part of the family business and we know that they will be with us, looking down and probably having a good old laugh throughout all of these events.

One Hundred years after the founding of my family's business on the Beautiful and majestic North Coast and I can wholeheartedly say that I'm looking forward to the next chapter in our History. In 1911 when my great uncle Peter opened his little shop in Stone Row, Coleraine, little did he know that he was laying the foundations for a famous brand that would live in the hearts of many. Anastasia carried the business through the tough times, as well as phases in our country's history that brought pain and suffering. She stayed focused throughout and looked to the future. She had faith in her family and a work ethic that focused on quality, tradition and meticulous attention to detail. That was her legacy to us and one for which we are all very grateful.

1st July 2011

77

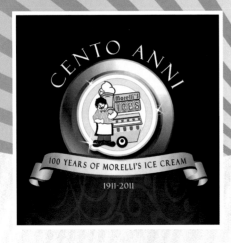

(Above) The commemorative Morelli's Cento Anni logo.

(Top right) Cento Anni planning meeting, Morelli's Portstewart, May 2011. From left to right: Nicole Morelli, Samantha Morelli, Tania Morelli-Whyte and Damian Morelli.

(Bottom right) Cento Anni planning meeting. From left to right: Angelo Morelli, Tania Morelli-Whyte, Arnaldo Morelli, Corrado Morelli, Nicole Morelli and Damian Morelli.

The three amigos, April 2011. From left to right: Guido, Corrado and Nino Morelli.

Young and Old. Guido, Nino and Corrado pictured with the two youngest members of the Morelli Family, Cadia Whyte and Nirucha Morelli.

CENTO ANNI

100 YEARS OF MORELLI'S ICE CREAM

1911-2011